NOELLE

Presented to

____

from

____

____

_____________________ 19 ____

The King's Numbers

A Bible Book about Counting

Concept by: Cheryl Rico and Ginger Knight
Illustrated by: Mary Grace Eubank
Text by: Mary Hollingsworth

Ft. Worth, TX 76137

The King's Numbers

Fort Worth, Texas 76137.

Library of Congress #87-43208

ISBN O-8344-0163-0

Published for Australia by
Lutheran Publishing House
205 Halifax Street
Adelaide, SA. 5000
ISBN 0-85910-477-X

Published for Canada by
R. G. Mitchell Family Books Inc.
565 Gordon Baker Road
Willowdale, Ontario
Canada M2H 2W2
ISBN 0-9693201-3-2

Printed in the United States of America.

10 9 8 7 6 5 4 3 2

Dear Parents,

How did you learn to count when you were a young child? Someone probably said, "How old are you?" and then helped you hold up one tiny finger. The next year you held up two fingers, and so on.

Counting is one of the very first educational skills a child learns, and it is basic to so many areas of life. We adults take for granted such skills as telling time, adding, subtracting and counting, but children must have help to develop their counting and mathematical skills.

The King's Numbers will entertain and delight your child while he learns about counting and about God's world at the same time. You can help him learn by reading the happy rhymes to him and then pointing to the groups of items on the page while he counts them aloud to you. "One . . . two . . . three. Look to see—Can you find the shepherds three?"

Counting is learned through repetition. Each page of *The King's Numbers* provides the child with an opportunity to count to the number being taught on that page over and over again. For instance, on the "nine" page the child can count nine birds, nine fishermen, nine fish, nine oars, nine ears, nine noses, etc. And all the time he'll be laughing at the colorful, happy art by one of the world-renown Sesame Street artists and learning about God's wonderful world.

The King's Numbers will amaze you in its ability to hold your child's attention as he learns to count. In the classic tradition of Dr. Seuss, Richard Scary and Mother Goose, this book will soon join the class of books that make learning really fun!

There's nothing like curling up in a big easy chair with your child and a good book. It's time to curl up with the King and His numbers.

The Publisher

Start with one
And count to ten;
Then start back with one again –
One zippy zebra
Two timid toucans
Three porky piggies
Four bashful bears
Five lucky lions
Six dreamy ducks
Seven mighty mice
Eight cuddly cats
Nine tardy turtles and
Ten funny fish.

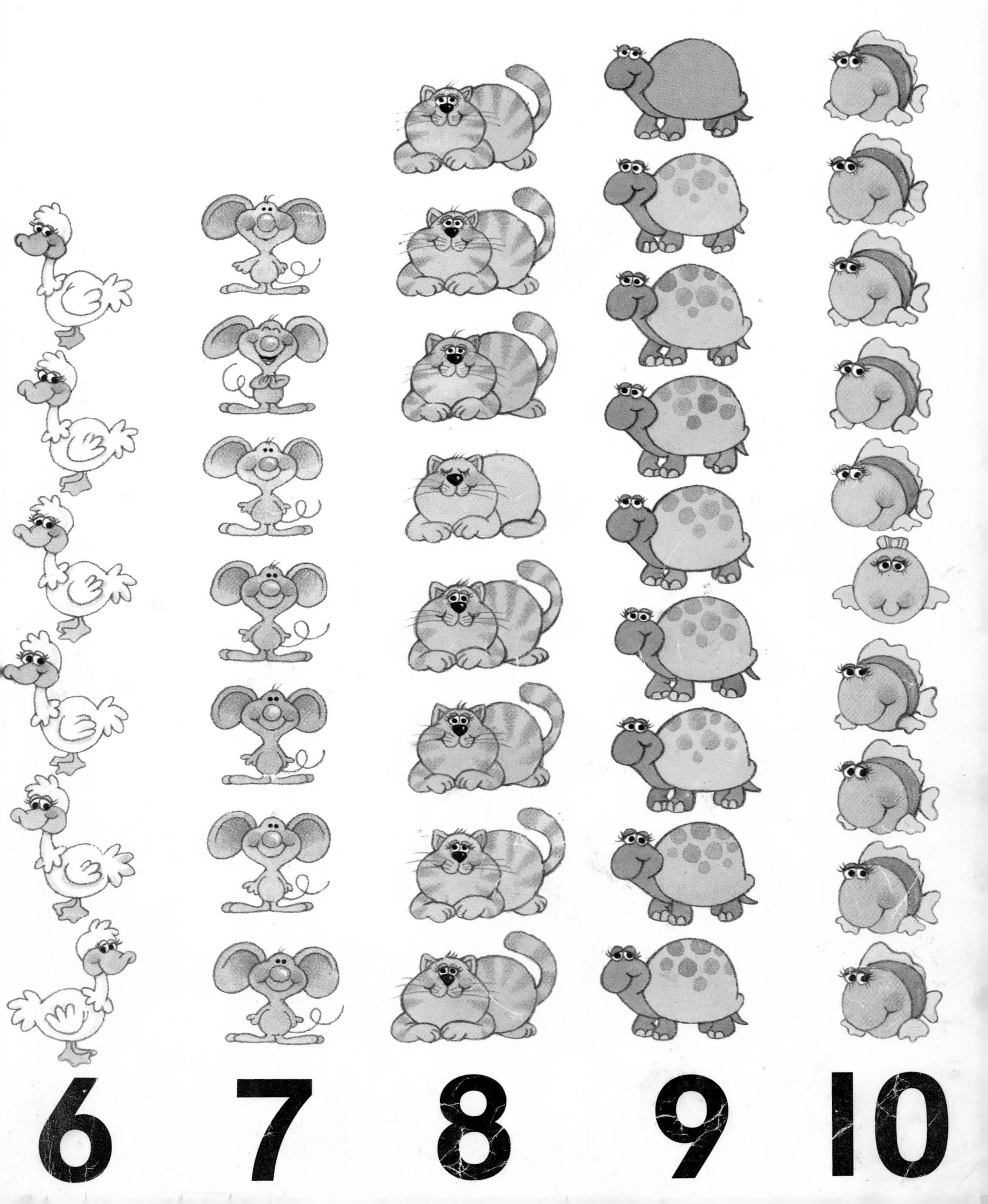
6
7
8
9
10

One . . . one . . . one.
Counting's fun!
God gave Eden a bright, warm sun.

2

Two . . . two . . . two.
Water's blue.
God saved creatures two by two.

3

One . . . two . . . three.
Look to see –
Can you find the shepherds three?

Four . . . four . . . four.
Tell me more!
Big bears sleep, but do they snore?

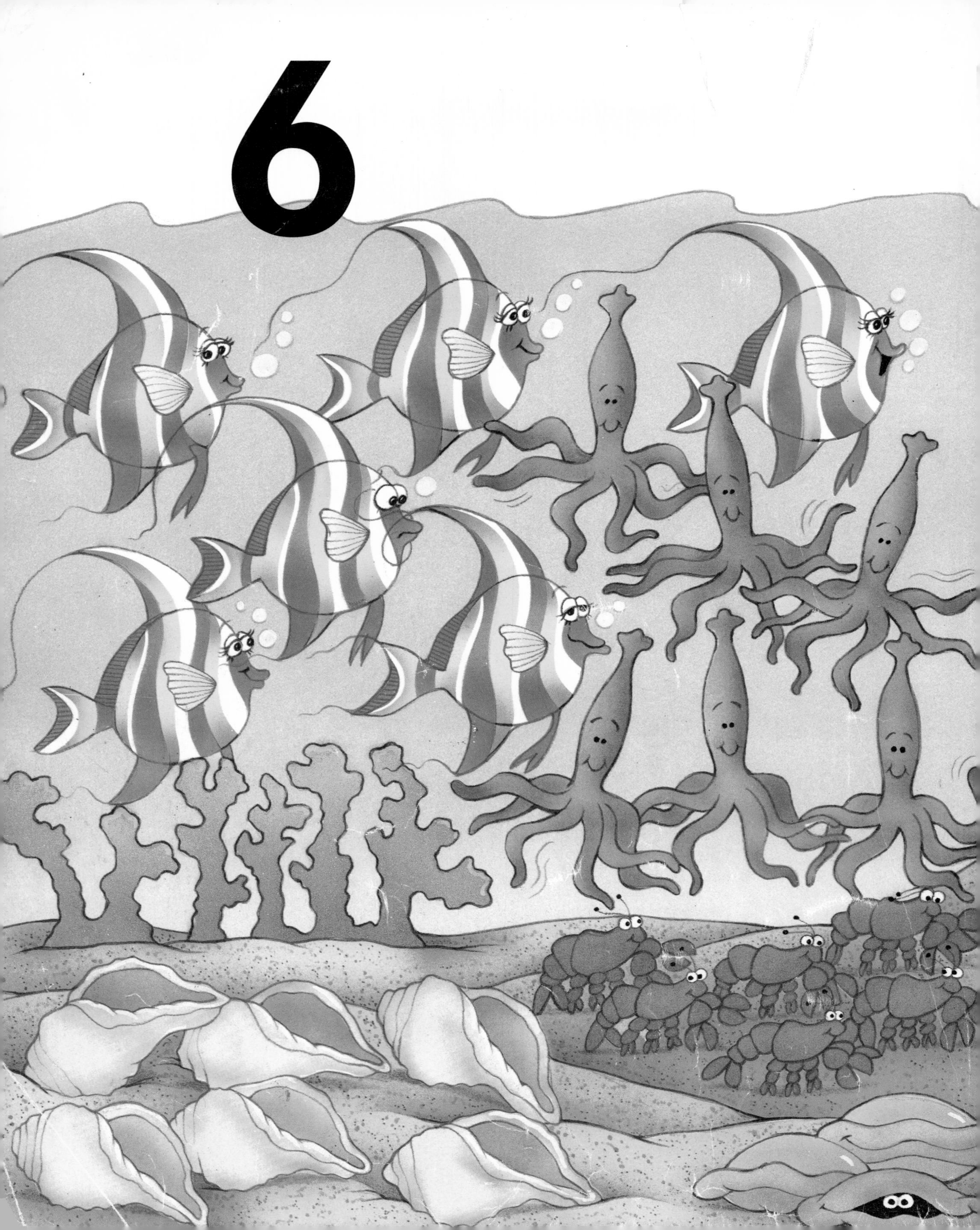
6

Six . . . six . . . six.
Seaweed's slick!
Do starfish sing or just do tricks?

Five . . . six . . . seven.
God's in heaven.
Next comes eight, nine, ten, eleven.

7

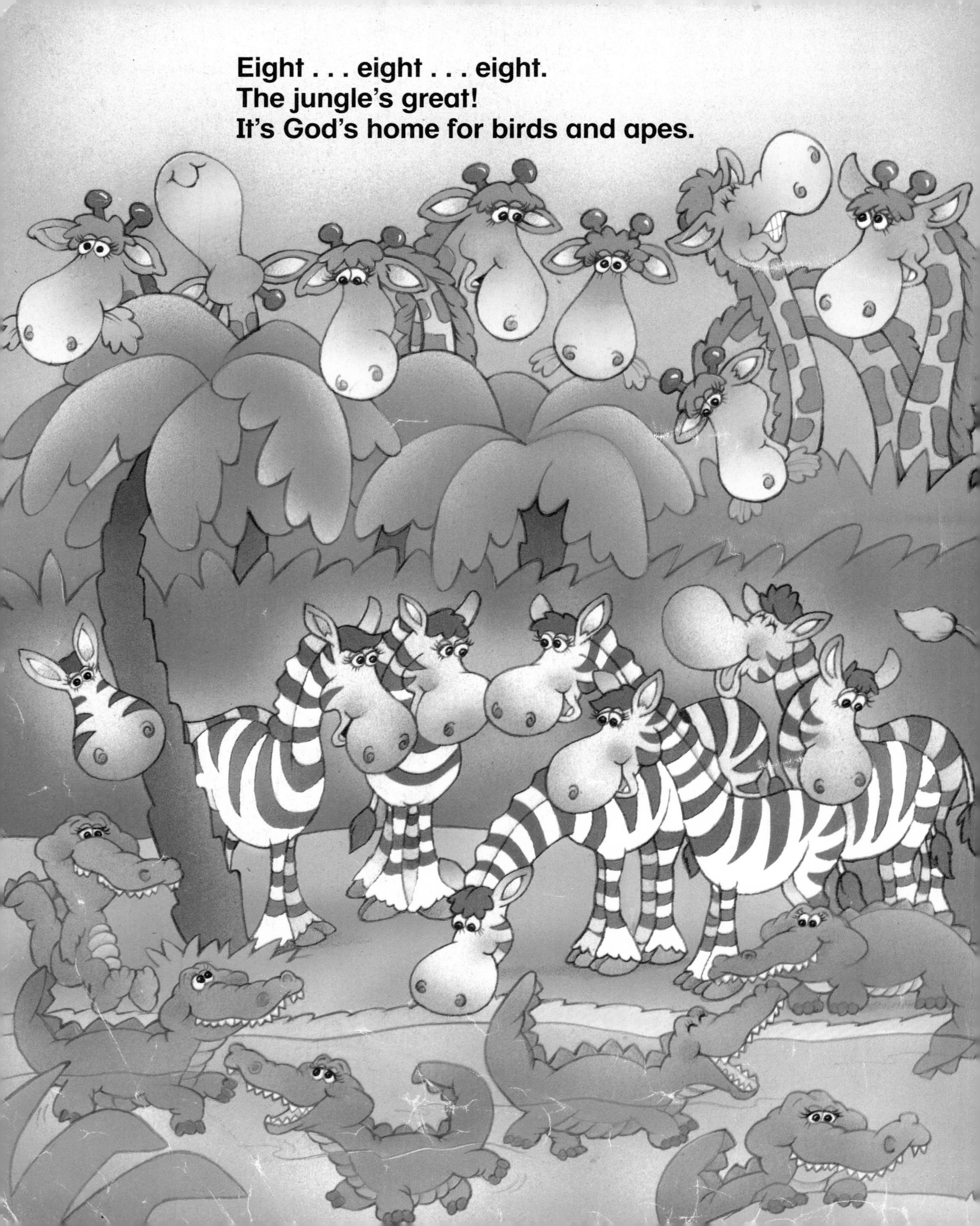

Eight . . . eight . . . eight.
The jungle's great!
It's God's home for birds and apes.

8

9

Nine . . . nine . . . nine.
The fishing's fine.
Jesus is a friend divine.

10
Eight . . . nine . . . ten.
Now, once again–
Count to ten and say, "Amen!"

You can count from one to ten.

Can you count back down again?

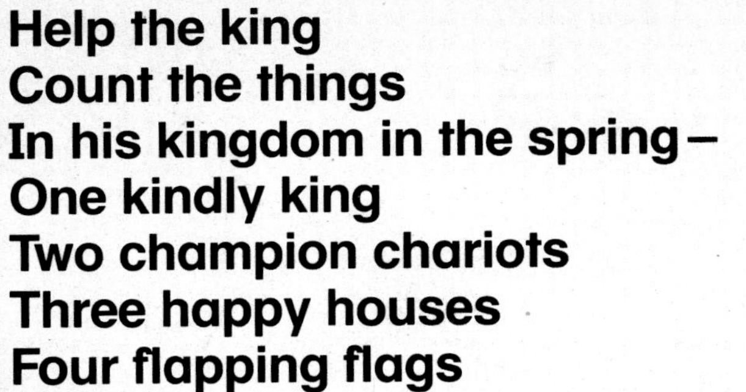

Help the king
Count the things
In his kingdom in the spring–
One kindly king
Two champion chariots
Three happy houses
Four flapping flags

Five smart soldiers
Six helpful horses
Seven tall trees
Eight stone steps.
Nine soft sheep and
Ten wide-open windows

Worthy Books for Children

Children of the King Series:

The King's Alphabet
A Bible Book about Letters

The King's Numbers
A Bible Book about Counting

Young Friends Series:

I'm No Ordinary Chicken
Nobody Likes Me
Will You Be My Friend?

Bible Books:

International Children's Bible
Read-n-Grow Picture Bible
What Does God Do?
Amy Grant's Heart-to-Heart Bible Stories